Gift of Mr. & Mrs. Meredith Wingert

Normandale Lutheran Church Library

EDINA, MINNESOTA 55436

The Life Cycle of a snapping turtle

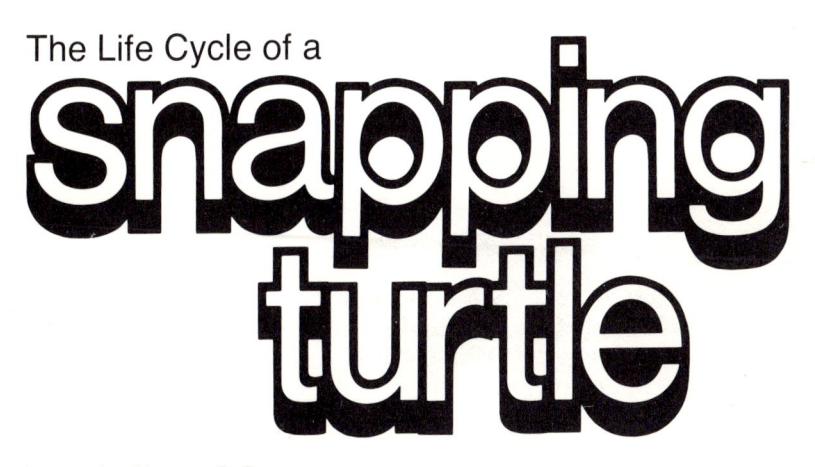

by Julian May
photographs by Allan Roberts
A CREATIVE EDUCATION MINI BOOK

Distributed Exclusively by
CHILDRENS PRESS, CHICAGO

Copyright © 1973 by Creative Educational Society, Inc. International copyrights reserved in all countries. No part of this book may be reproduced in any form, except for reviews, without permission in writing from the publisher. Printed in the United States.

ISBN: 0-87191-239-2
Library of Congress Catalog Card Number: 73-1061

Contents

- 6   The snapper
- 12   Mother lays eggs
- 16   Eggs hatch
- 22   Survival
- 27   Different kinds
- 31   Range and lifespan

the life cycle of a snapping turtle

the snapper

"Don't come too close!"

This seems to be what the snapping turtle is saying. It opens its jaws and hisses loudly. Its head darts forward and its mouth snaps shut. The large mouth has no teeth, but its bony edges are as sharp as knives.

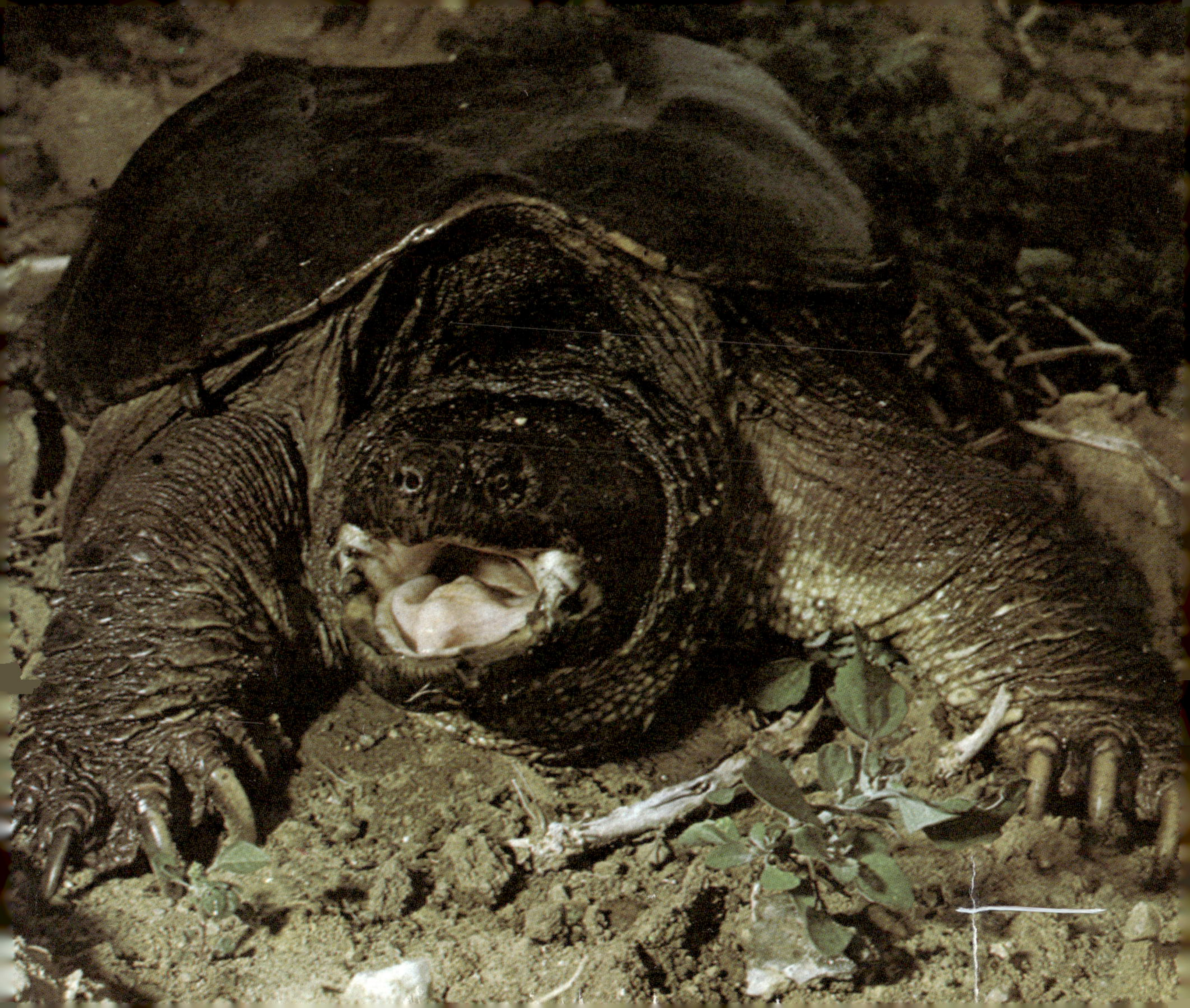

Once the turtle bites, it hangs on tightly. But it is not true that it will only let go when the sun goes down, or when it thunders. It lets go when it wants to. Even tiny snapping turtles will bite hard. Huge old adults can do serious harm to the hands and feet of careless persons. But the turtle does not look for trouble. It just wants to be left alone. Its sharp jaws help it catch food.

The snapping turtle is a reptile, related to snakes and lizards. Like them, it is a "cold-blooded" animal. This means that its body is just about as warm or as cold as the air or water around it. Turtles cannot warm themselves by eating food and turning it into heat energy, as birds and mammals can. In cold weather a turtle slows down. In winter, it hibernates, or falls into a deep sleep.

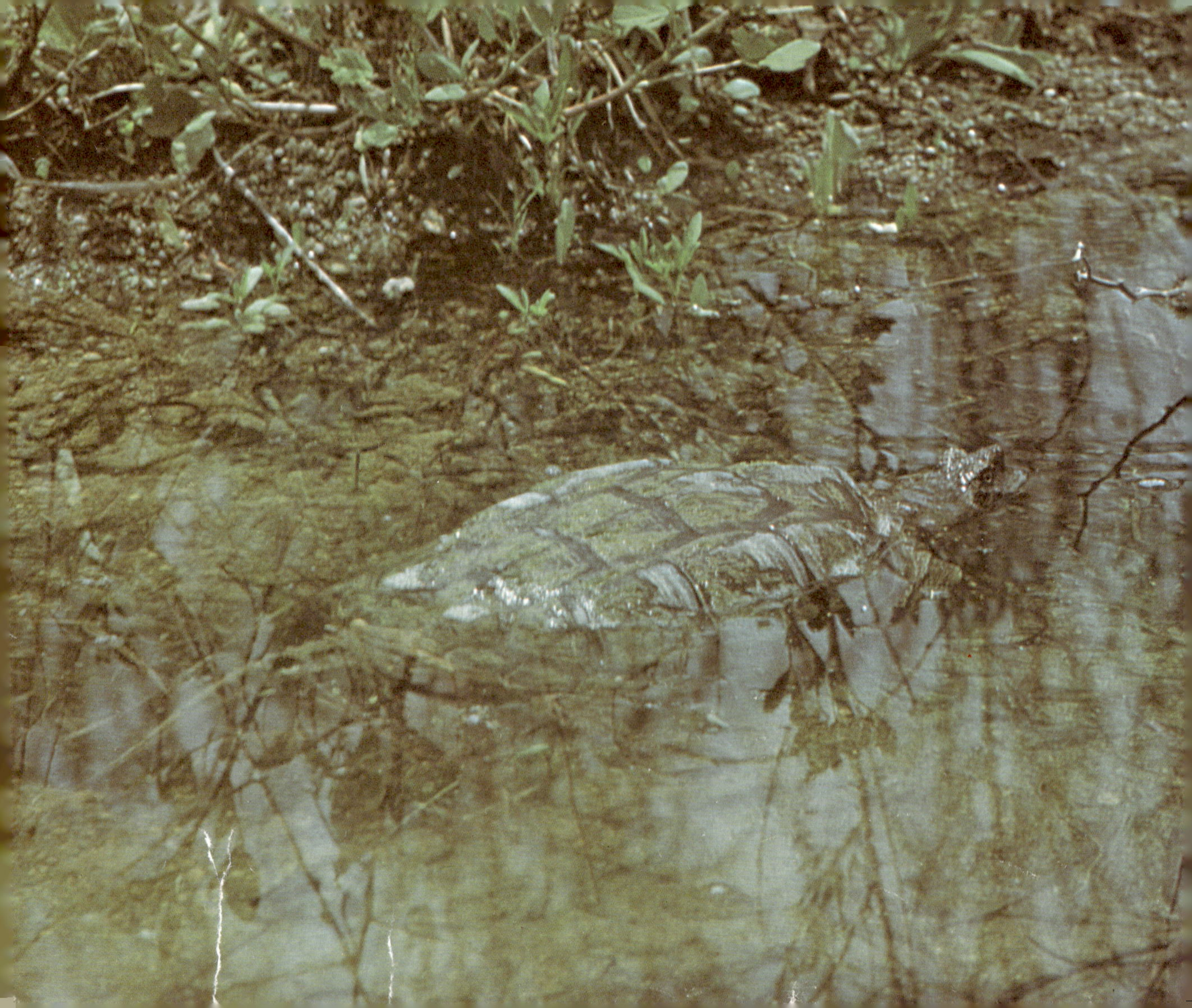

The snapping turtle lives mostly in the water. Sometimes it comes out onto land, especially in spring. Ponds, city lagoons, lakes, swamps, and slow-flowing streams are homes to snappers. The turtles can also live in the part-fresh, part-salty waters of marshes along the sea. Snappers spend the winter in holes in the bank of a stream, or buried in mud on the bottom of a pond. They come out when spring warms the water.

mother lays eggs

The mother turtle usually lays her eggs in late spring, when it is quite warm. She must find a sunny spot to build her nest. The sun will heat and hatch her eggs.

With her hind feet, she digs a hole. Then she sits in it and lays the eggs from an opening beneath her tail. Each egg is round, about an inch wide. It has a firm shell, something like white plastic.

Inside each egg is a yolk, something like that in a hen's egg. The yolk is food for a tiny clump of growing cells that will become a baby turtle. As the sun warms the egg, the turtle grows a heart, lungs, a small brain, stomach, muscles, skin, and bones. It even grows a tiny shell. The yolk grows smaller and smaller. It is used up in making the young turtle's body.

From 20 to 30 eggs are laid. Then the mother scratches earth and leaves over them. Unless the eggs are hidden carefully, they may be dug up and eaten by animals. Foxes and skunks love turtle eggs.

The mother takes no further care of her eggs. They must hatch by themselves. If they were laid in June, the eggs will hatch in late September. In the North, the mother lays her eggs in fall and they hatch in spring.

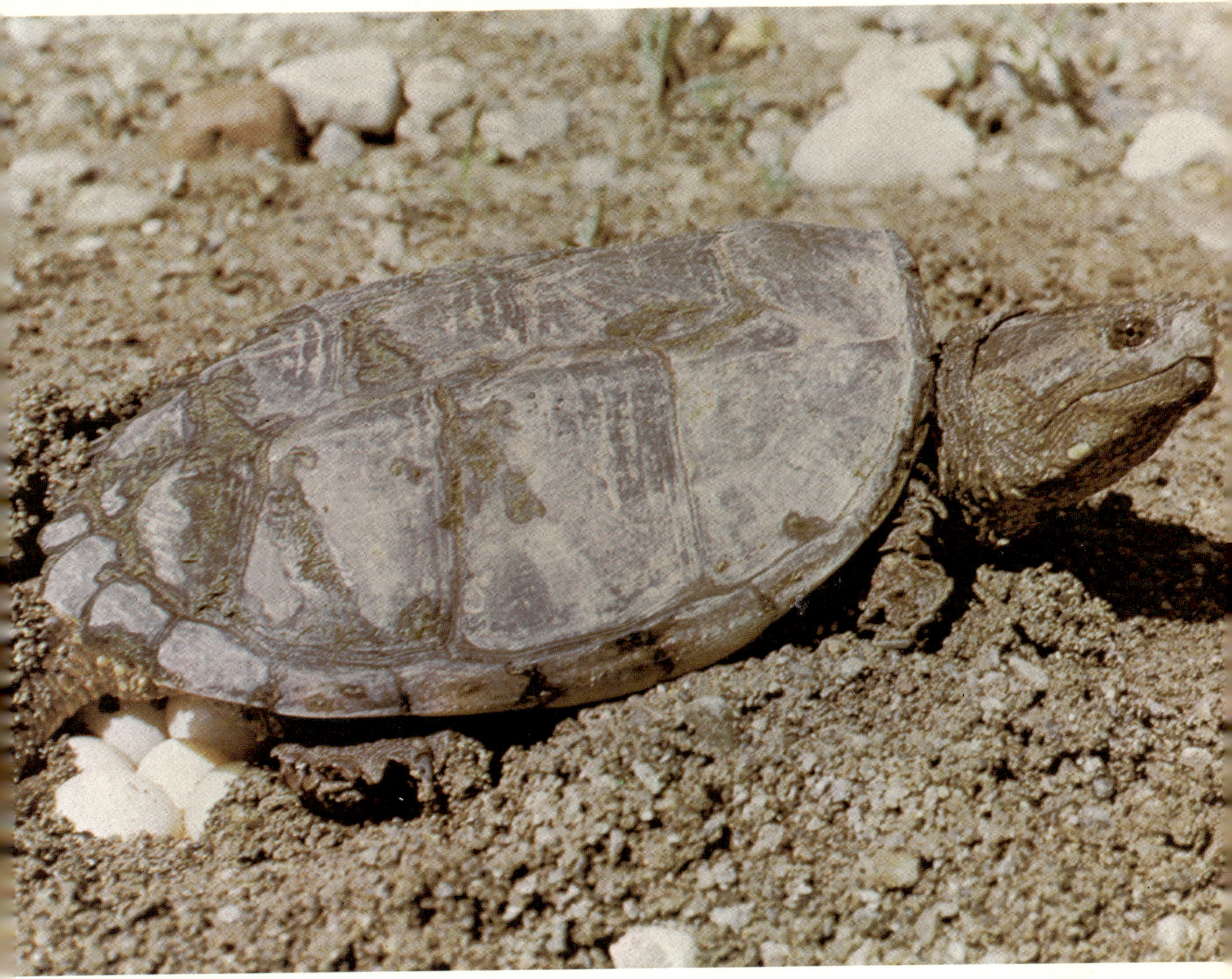

eggs hatch

If the turtle's eggs escape being eaten by some hungry animal, the young will hatch—all at about the same time.

They dig up through the soft earth and immediately start to crawl toward water.

Newly hatched snapping turtles are often black or very dark brown, with light spots around the edge of the shell. The upper shell is quite rough.

The babies have very long tails. They can be told from other kinds of young turtles by the small, cross-shaped under-shell, or plastron. The upper shell is called a carapace. Both shells are still soft.

Soon after hatching, the babies seek water. They often march in a group. At this time they are in great danger. Crows, hawks, herons, and other birds wait to catch them and gulp them down.

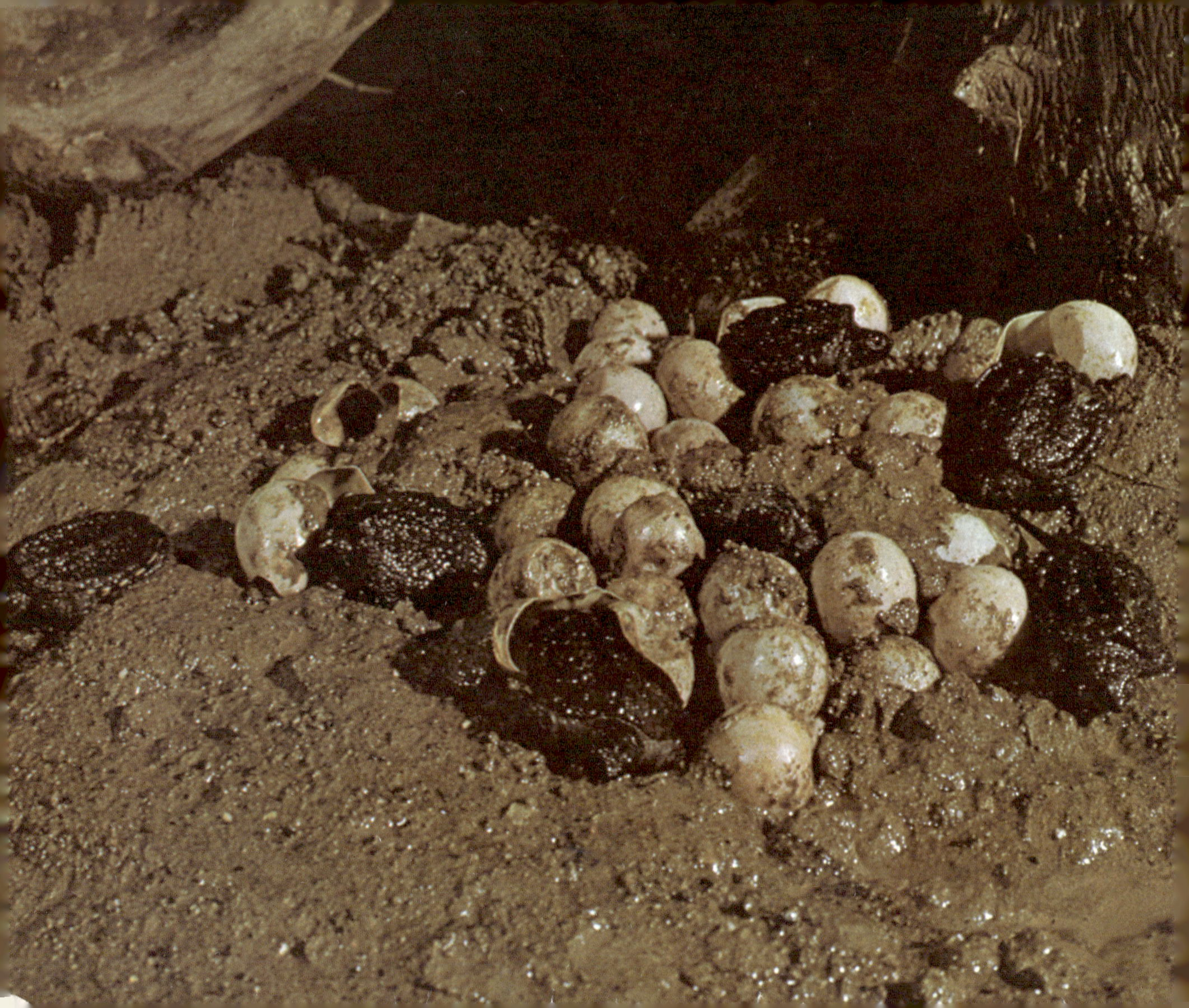

Mammals such as dogs, coyotes, raccoons, foxes, and skunks also will try to eat them while they are on land. And when they reach the water, they may be taken by large fish or even by adult snapping turtles. The mother turtle lays many eggs because only a few of the babies will live to grow up.

Once in water, the babies seek food. They eat small water animals, earthworms, plants, and dead animals.

Snappers do not seem to be very good swimmers. They are more likely to walk about on the bottom, or hide among the plants or rocks waiting for prey. They can stay under water for a long time. But they do not breathe in water, like a fish. They must come up for air, because they breathe with lungs.

Snappers do not lie about in the sun, as many kinds of turtles do, nor do they gather in groups.

Snapping turtles live mostly by themselves, quietly searching for food and growing larger and larger. Their feet, armed with claws, help them dig in the mud. They can pull in their legs and head if danger threatens, but the plastron does not protect all of the underside of the turtle. It seems "too small" for the animal. On the other hand, the small plastron lets the turtle move about rapidly.

Even large snappers can run quickly.

survival

The snapping turtle is a predator—an animal that lives by catching and eating other creatures. It lies in wait, half-buried in the mud, and grabs its prey with a swift lunge. The turtle in the picture has captured a water snake, another reptile that swims. Snapping turtles also eat fish, frogs, crayfish, snails, and even young ducks. Fishermen know they are great bait-stealers.

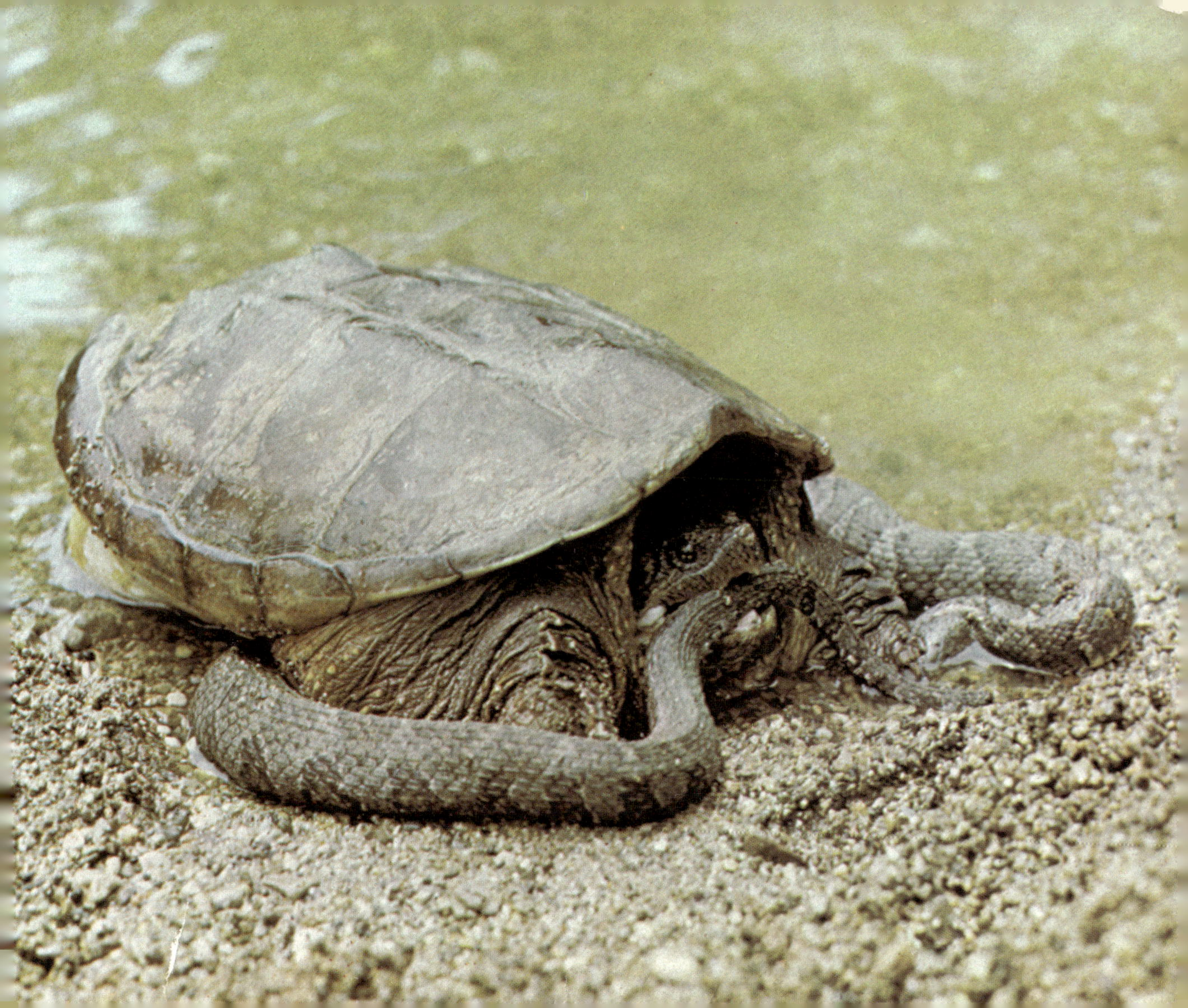

A full-grown snapping turtle is a muddy gray-green color. Young turtles have ridges on their shells. Old adults have smooth shells that are often overgrown with moss-like algae plants.

The carapace of an adult is 8 to 18 inches long. The animal may weigh from 10 to more than 40 pounds. It has few enemies besides man.

Males and females look much the same.

Some people value the snapping turtle for its meat, which makes a delicious soup. It is also important to man because of the way it hunts. By eating other animals, it helps prevent them from becoming too numerous. Snappers are also scavengers, or eaters of dead things, helping to keep waters clean.

Snapping turtle eggs and babies are also food for birds and mammals.

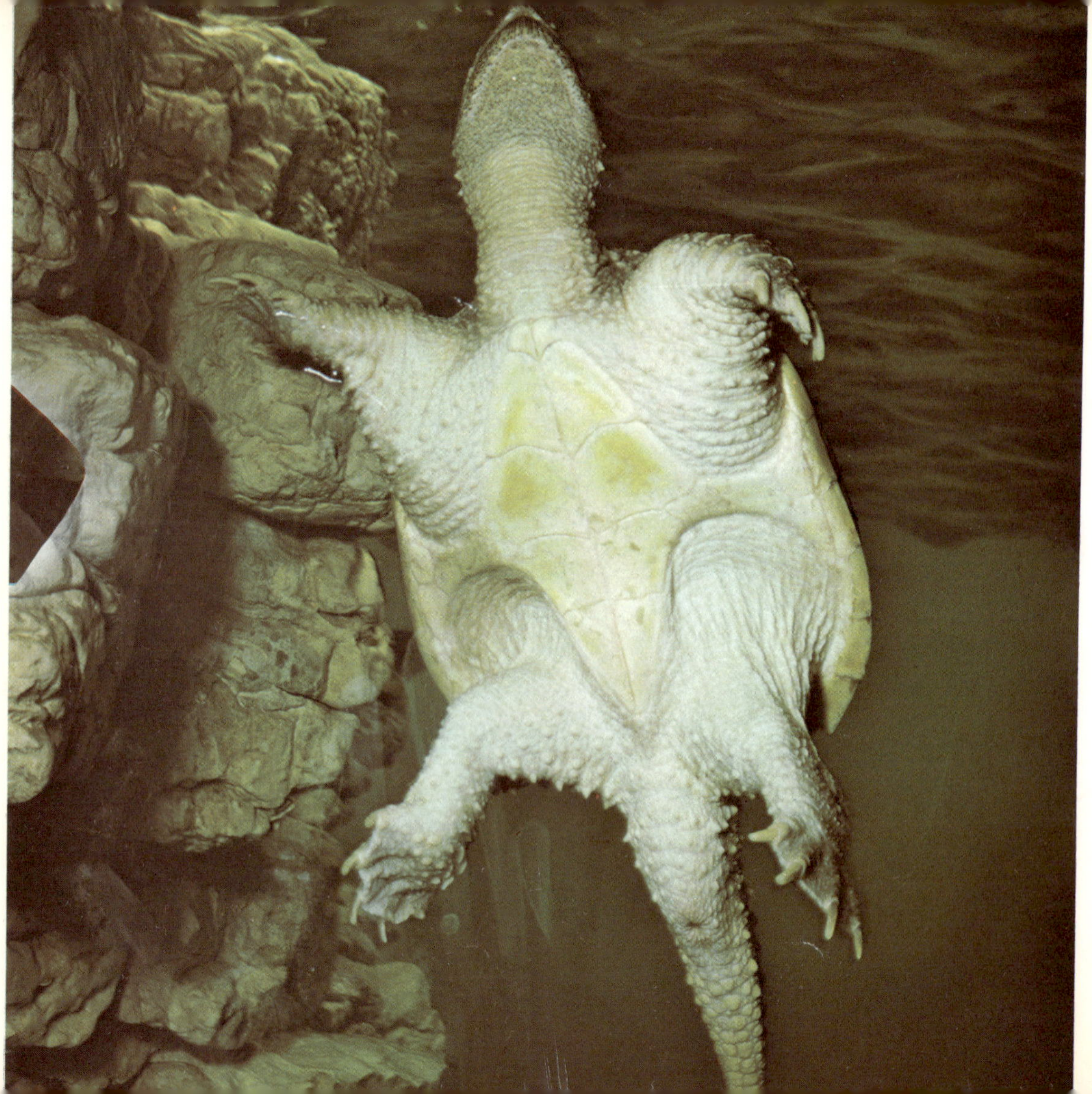

different kinds

The common snapping turtle lives from southern Nova Scotia westward to the Rocky Mountains, and southward to Texas and the Gulf States. It is not found west of the Rocky Mountains.

The picture shows the cross-shaped plastron, or under-shell, of an adult snapping turtle.

The alligator snapping turtle lives in the Mississippi Valley, from Illinois and Kansas southward to the Gulf of Mexico. It also dwells in warm, slow-moving rivers of Florida and Georgia.

It is hard for a person who is not a scientist to tell a young alligator snapper from a common snapper. The alligator snapper has a very rough shell, a hooked beak, and a very long tail.

An adult alligator snapping turtle may be more than two feet long and weigh more than 200 pounds. It does not have the "sawtooth" tail of the common snapper.

The alligator snapper is the largest turtle in North America—and one of the largest anywhere in the world. Sometimes it waits with its mouth open, wiggling its small, wormlike tongue as a bait for fishes. Its jaws can cause serious injury to man.

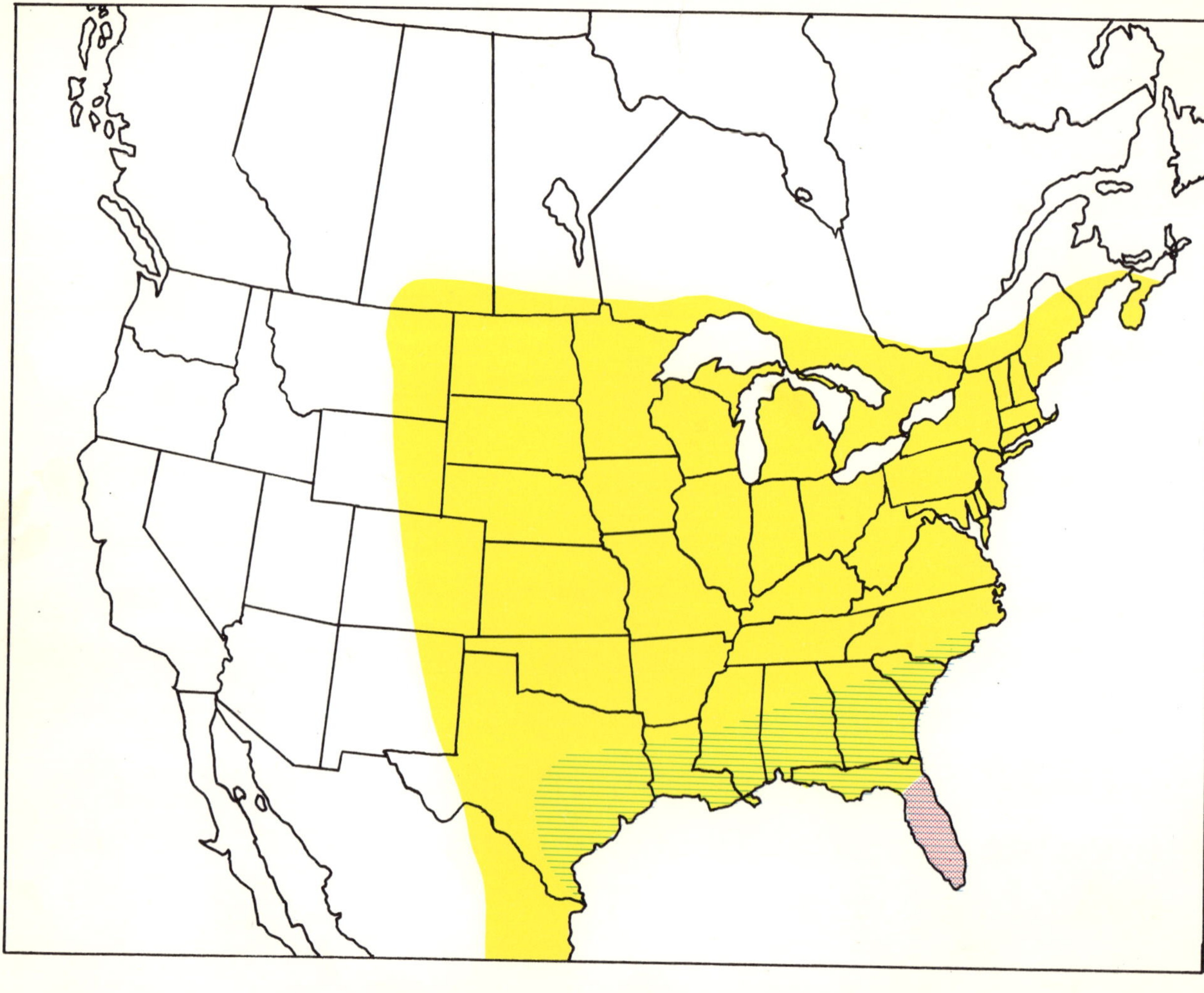

☐ COMMON SNAPPING TURTLE

☐ ALLIGATOR SNAPPING TURTLE

☐ FLORIDA SNAPPING TURTLE

range and lifespan

The map shows the range, or place where different kinds of snapping turtles live. They cannot live in places where there are not enough sunny days to warm and hatch the eggs, nor can they cross hot deserts. Too much heat and dryness will kill a snapping turtle.

Once a snapping turtle survives to adulthood, it may live more than 40 years. Alligator snappers may live more than 60 years.

Other Creative Mini Books

Life Cycles

Life Cycle of a Bullfrog
Life Cycle of a Raccoon
Life Cycle of an Opossum
Life Cycle of a Moth
Life Cycle of a Rabbit
Life Cycle of a Fox
Life Cycle of a Turtle
Life Cycle of a Butterfly

World We Know

Fishes We Know
Birds We Know
Reptiles We Know
Mammals We Know
Insects We Know

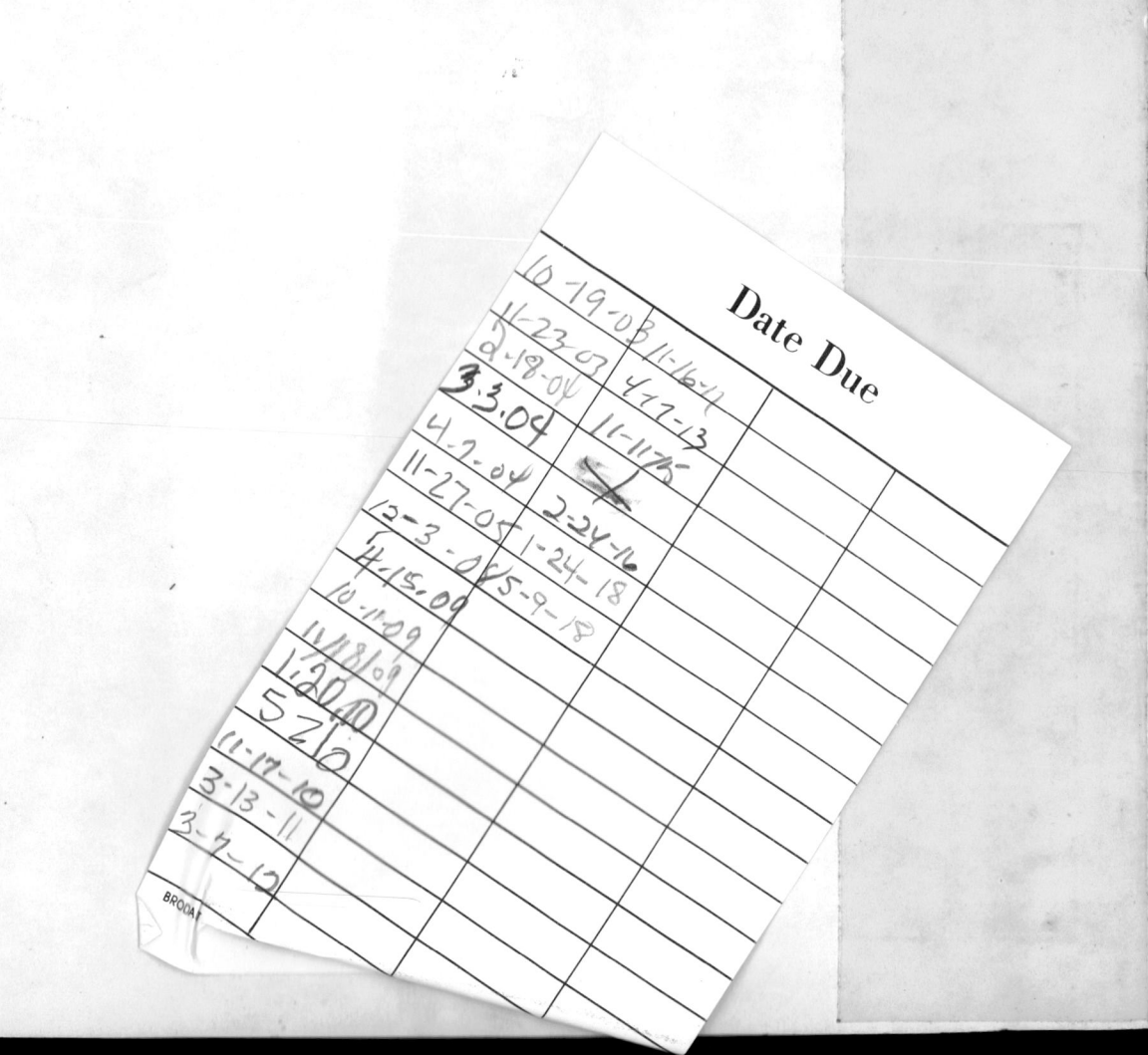

Date Due				
10-19-03	11-16-07			
11-23-03				
2-18-04	4-17-13			
3-3-04	11-11-15			
4-2-04				
11-27-04	2-24-16			
12-3-05	1-24-18			
4-15-09	5-9-18			
10-1-09				
11/18/09				
1:20 m				
5-2-10				
11-17-10				
3-13-11				
3-7-12				